The Horse Lover's Companion

Dedication
For Elwyn, with gratitude for his
boundless enthusiasm and encouragement
'I can no other answer make but thanks,
and thanks, and ever thanks.'
(*Twelfth Night*)

Text and captions Judith Draper

Astrology Louise Houghton

Editor Fleur Robertson

Design Claire Leighton

Photography Bob Langrish

Illustrations Ann Carley; Terry Burton, courtesy of
Bernard Thornton Artists, London
(astrological cartoons)

Production Ruth Arthur; Sally Connolly,
Neil Randles, Jonathan Tickner

Director of Production Gerald Hughes

Acknowledgement is made to Stanley Paul,
publishers of *Riding The True Techniques* by Lucy Rees

CLB 3477
This edition published in 1995
© 1994 Colour Library Books Ltd, Godalming, Surrey, UK
Colour separations by Scantrans PTE Ltd, Singapore
Printed in Italy
ISBN 1-85833-148-X

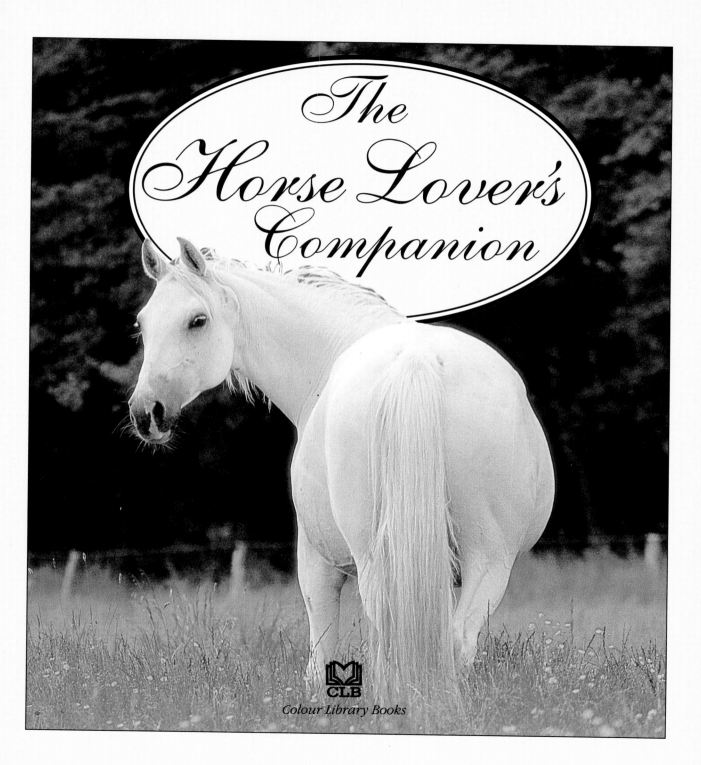

The Horse Lover's Companion

CLB
Colour Library Books

~ *Introduction* ~

The Horse Lover's Companion is for horse lovers everywhere, whether or not they own a horse. In the following pages there is a wealth of horses. Sensitively drawn and photographed, they come together to form a wonderful collection, appealing to the wide range of their admirers, from the fans of the smallest ponies, such as the ever-popular Shetland, and admirers of the elegant Thoroughbred and majestic Arabian, to lovers of the mighty workhorses, such as the noble Shire. Especially useful as a place to record the special days of family and friends – and horses! – this unique book is also a treasury of intriguing horsey information, fascinating to read wherever the pages fall open.

Beautiful to look at and easy to use, *The Horse Lover's Companion* is an essential for all those happy people who are 'crazy about horses'.

Welsh pony mares with their foals make a delightful picture in a summer meadow.

~ *January* ~

*Men are generally more careful of the breed of their horses
and dogs than of their children.*

Reflexions and Maxims
William Penn (1644-1718)

January horses are quiet and reliable. Like these Haflinger ponies, they are conscientious workers.

~ January ~

~ 1 ~

~ 2 ~

~ 3 ~

~ 4 ~

~ 5 ~

~ 6 ~

~ 7 ~

HORSE RHYMES

There is a popular old rhyme that goes: 'Ride a cock-horse to Banbury Cross, To see a fine lady upon a white horse ...' A cock horse (or trace horse) was a sturdy animal specially employed to help horse-drawn vehicles to surmount especially steep hills. The horse would be stationed at the foot of the hill ready to be hitched in front of any team that needed assistance. One of the best known of London's cock horses of this century was Wimbledon Jack. In one six-month period, he is said to have made nearly 2,000 journeys up Wimbledon Hill, London.

HORSE HEROES
Copenhagen

The Duke of Wellington's charger Copenhagen was a horse of phenomenal stamina and became a household name after the Battle of Waterloo (June 18, 1815). The day before the battle he carried the Iron Duke for 60 miles. On the day of the battle Wellington was in the saddle for more than 15 hours. When he dismounted, Copenhagen is reputed to have still had sufficient energy to kick out with his hindfeet, narrowly missing the Duke's head. Copenhagen was a chestnut grandson of the great racehorse Eclipse and raced himself before passing into the Duke's possession. He took his name from the exploits of his dam, Lady Catherine, who carried General Grosvenor at the Siege of Copenhagen and was in foal when she departed for England. Copenhagen was 28 when he died in 1836. He was buried at the Duke's home, Stratfield Saye, with full military honours. On his gravestone is the inscription:
'God's humble instrument, though meaner clay, Should share the glory of that glorious day.'

His pricked ears show that this foal's attention is focused on the photographer.

A Dutch Heavy Draught mare keeps a watchful eye on her long-legged offspring.

~ January ~

~ 8 ~

~ 9 ~

~ 10 ~

~ 11 ~

~ 12 ~

~ 13 ~

~ 14 ~

PHANTOM HORSES

Sir Francis Drake is said to haunt the Tavistock-to-Plymouth road driving a hearse drawn by four headless horses. Sir Thomas Boleyn, the father of Anne Boleyn, ill-fated wife of Henry VIII, is reputed to drive a coach drawn by four headless horses on the roads near his East Anglian home. Legend has it that Sir Thomas is doomed for a thousand years to haunt the Norfolk countryside.

Catch as catch can!

HORSE LEGENDS

In parts of England there are large representations of horses, some thought to date from pre-Roman times, cut in hillsides. The Uffington White Horse in Berkshire bears a close resemblance to the horse that featured on Celtic coins from around 150 BC. These hill carvings are believed to be part of Celtic horse worship.

HORSE SENSE

When steam trams first appeared on the streets of San Francisco towards the end of the 19th century the horses were terrified. To alleviate the ensuing pandemonium in the city, a man called S.R. Mathewson invented an 'equine-friendly' tram. Gas-fired and built in the form of a horse, it was apparently soon accepted by the real horses, who worked alongside it quite happily.

The beautiful Arabian, noted for its intelligent, expressive head.

~ January ~

~ 15 ~

~ 16 ~

~ 17 ~

~ 18 ~

~ 19 ~

~ 20 ~

~ 21 ~

HORSE FACTS

A horse's age can be told, with varying degrees of accuracy, from its teeth. In a young horse age can be determined by the number of temporary or permanent teeth it has (a 'full mouth' contains 12 incisors and 24 molars, plus four tusk-like teeth called tushes which are normally only seen in male horses), and by marks on the grinding surfaces or 'tables' of the teeth. After the age of seven it becomes more difficult to make an accurate calculation and a horse over seven is said to be 'aged'. In older horses the degree of wear and the change in the angle of the teeth make it possible to estimate the age.

RECORD-BREAKING HORSES

The oldest recorded age for a horse is 62. Old Billy, probably a mixture of Cleveland and eastern blood, was born in Lancashire in 1760. He was at work on the canals until 1819 and died on November 27, 1822.

By nature herbivores, horses and ponies find hay a palatable substitute for fresh grass.

Miniature horses make engaging pets, but they need just as much care as their bigger relatives.

HORSE FACTS

It is rare for horses to give birth to twins. The mare's uterus is designed for only one foetus, so when two are present, there is such a shortage of space that it usually causes one or both to be either aborted or re-absorbed.

~ 22 ~

~ 23 ~

~ 24 ~

HORSE SCANDALS

A thoroughbred called Running Rein holds the distinction of being the only horse to have won the Epsom Derby, which is restricted to three-year-olds, and then been disqualified for being the wrong age. In 1944, soon after the colt passed the winning post three-quarters of a length in front of the field, an objection was lodged on the suspicion he was a 'ringer': a look-alike substituted for the real horse. It was subsequently proved that Running Rein was in fact a four-year-old horse called Maccabeus. The plot, with more ramifications than any modern work of crime fiction, was devised by a clever and unscrupulous villain named Abraham Levi Goodman, who had hoped to bring off a lucrative betting coup.

~ 25 ~

~ 26 ~

~ 27 ~

~ 28 ~

Twins in horses are very rare.

~ January ~

~ 29 ~

~ 30 ~

~ 31 ~

The Akhal-Teke, with its striking metallic-sheen coat, comes from Turkmenistan.

MYTHOLOGICAL HORSES

According to the Iliad, Xanthus was the horse of Archilles, the offspring of Zephyrus, the west wind, and Podarge, the harpy, a winged monster with the head and breasts of a woman. The goddess Here endowed Xanthus with the power of human speech, but the Furies struck him dumb after he foretold that Achilles would fall in battle to a god and a man. Achilles subsequently slew Hector, but later died at the hands of Apollo and Paris.

HORSE FACTS

Apart from being a mythological one-horned animal, a unicorn is also the name of a three-horse team of driven horses. Two wheelers are harnessed side by side immediately in front of the vehicle, with a single leader in front.

At its most vulnerable when drinking, the horse uses its highly sensitive ears to detect danger.

~ *February* ~

With flowing tail and flying mane,
Wide nostrils, never stretched by pain,
Mouths bloodless to the bit or rein,
And feet that iron never shod,
And flanks unscar'd by spur or rod
A thousand horses – the wild – the free –
Like waves that follow o'er the sea,
Came thickly thundering on.'

Mazeppa
Lord Byron (1788-1824)

Intelligent and independent, February horses often make good mounts for the sport of endurance riding.

~ *February* ~

~ 1 ~

~ 2 ~

~ 3 ~

ERUDITE HORSES

Philip Astley, founder of the first circus in London in 1779, had a horse called Billy, advertised as 'The Little Learned Military Horse', who could unsaddle himself, wash his feet in a bucket, perform various mental feats and wait at table.

~ 4 ~

~ 5 ~

~ 6 ~

~ 7 ~

HORSE LOVERS

Robert Hardy
(b.1925)
British actor Robert Hardy has had a varied career, appearing in everything from Shakespeare to films such as The Spy Who Came in from the Cold. *But the performance which probably introduced him to the widest audience was as the veterinary surgeon Siegfried Farnon in* All Creatures Great and Small, *the long-running TV series based on James Herriot's books. Handling horses on screen is no problem for Robert Hardy, because he has ridden since he was a child, even on one memorable occasion trying his hand at point-to-pointing. Horses have always been very much a part of the Hardy family's lives.*

Two of Britain's renowned breeds: the Shire (left) and the Suffolk Punch.

HORSE SENSE

Like humans, the horse often has to fashion his diet according to his environment. In the desert, horses of the Bedouin will drink camels' milk and have been known to eat anything from dates and cooked meats to locusts.

Despite their great size heavy horses are noted for their gentleness and docility.

~ 8 ~

~ 9 ~

HORSE SUPERSTITIONS

In the English county off Lincolnshire, if you see a white dog, you should stay silent until you have also seen a white horse.

~ 10 ~

~ 11 ~

~ 12 ~

HORSE LEAPS

According to legend, a Dorset man called 'Conjuring' John Mintern ('conjuring' signified that he was thought to be in league with the Devil) once jumped his horse off Batcombe Hill, knocking the top off the church tower in the process.

~ 13 ~

~ 14 ~

An irresistible Welsh foal.

HORSESHOES

According to legend, St Dunstan (924-988), famous for his skill as a farrier, was one day asked by the Devil to shoe him. Aware of the identity of his visitor, the wily Dunstan tied him to the wall and deliberately inflicted so much pain during the shoeing that the Devil begged for mercy. Dunstan eventually released him, but not before extracting an assurance that he would never again enter any place where a horseshoe was displayed.

Rich rolling grassland: the natural environment for a mare and foal.

~ 15 ~

~ 16 ~

~ 17 ~

~ 18 ~

~ 19 ~

~ 20 ~

~ 21 ~

RECORD-BREAKING HORSES

The oldest recorded age for a thoroughbred racehorse is 42, set by an Australian gelding called Tango Duke who was foaled in 1935 and died on January 25, 1978.

HORSE HEROINES
Kincsem

Kincsem, a thoroughbred mare foaled at the Hungarian National Stud in 1874, holds perhaps the most remarkable racing record in Turf history. She ran ten times as a two-year-old, 17 as a three-year-old, 15 as a four-year-old and 12 as a five-year-old. She was unbeaten in all 54 starts at all distances from under five furlongs to two-and-a-half miles. She raced in Austria, England, Germany, Hungary, France and Czechoslovakia, and seemed to thrive on the long train journeys which were extremely arduous at that time. She was devoted to her lad Frankie and her pet cat, and would go anywhere she was asked, provided they accompanied her.

Foals love to frisk and play though they rarely stray far from their dams.

In the wild a fine stallion, such as this Arabian, could command a large group of mares.

~ *February* ~

~ 22 ~

HORSE POWER

The horse has been revered since pagan times, doubtless because of the power with which he imbues his rider. Perhaps the most widely known equestrian protector-figure is St George, who became patron saint of many kingdoms, including Portugal, Aragon, the German Empire and England. St George is depicted as the archetypal knight, slaying the dragon and rescuing the maiden in distress.

~ 23 ~

~ 24 ~

HORSE LEGENDS

According to legend, the Chinese calendar began when Buddha invited all the animals to celebrate the first New Year with him. The seventh to respond was the horse, who accordingly had the seventh year of the 12-year calendar named after him. People born in the Chinese Year of the Horse are said to be intelligent, selfish, quick-witted, tactless, eloquent – and poor marriage partners!

~ 25 ~

~ 26 ~

~ 27 ~

~ 28/29 ~

For centuries wild ponies have bred on Chincoteague and Assateague islands, off the coast of Virginia.

A charming Chincoteague mare, heavily in foal.

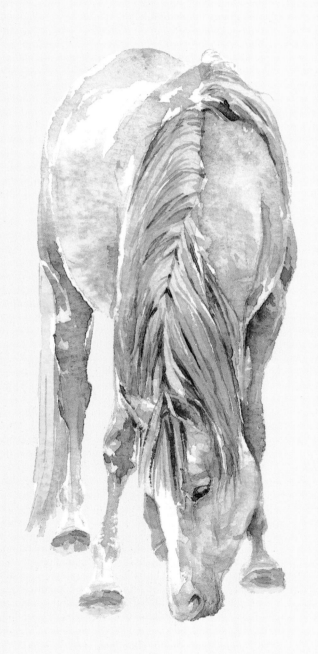

~ *March* ~

To God I speak Spanish, to women Italian, to men French,
and to my horse – German.

Attributed to Charles V (1500-1558)

The March horse is kind and graceful, often possessing large, expressive eyes.

~ 1 ~

~ 2 ~

~ 3 ~

~ 4 ~

~ 5 ~

~ 6 ~

~ 7 ~

RECORD-BREAKING HORSES

In 1865 Gladiateur, one of the greatest racehorses ever bred in France, became the first horse in history to win the English Triple Crown (the 2,000 Guineas, the Derby and the St Leger) and the French Derby (the Grand Prix de Paris). It is a record which has never been equalled. The style with which Gladiateur defeated his English rivals earned him the nickname 'The Avenger of Waterloo'. He is commemorated in bronze at Longchamp racecourse.

PHANTOM HORSES

Horses have long been associated with the supernatural. Writing nearly 2,000 years ago, the Greek traveller and geographer Pausanias (c. AD 150) claimed that the Olympian hippodrome was haunted by a horse ghost which caused racehorses to shy, resulting in many fatal chariot crashes.

HORSE LOVERS

Queen Elizabeth II
(b. April 21, 1926)

The Queen of England is renowned for her interest in and knowledge of horses, in particular, bloodstock. The Queen learnt to ride as a child, and later took over the running of the Royal studs of Sandringham and Wolferton, where she has produced many fine racehorses. In the week of her coronation (June 2, 1953) she nearly won the blue riband of flat racing, the Epsom Derby, with her colt Aureole. He eventually finished runner-up to Pinza. Aureole spent his stud career at Wolferton, and from the wooden shelter in his field, in view of the railway which brought visitors to the royal estate, he used to indulge in train spotting. He learnt to distinguish at long range between trains which brought only human visitors and those carrying mares bound for the stud. The purely passenger trains he would ignore. The others, however, he always greeted from across his paddock with welcoming neighs.

Siesta time for a young foal.

Selective breeding has made the twentieth-century warmblood the world's leading competition horse.

~ March ~

~ 8 ~

~ 9 ~

~ 10 ~

~ 11 ~

~ 12 ~

~ 13 ~

~ 14 ~

HORSE POWER

There were an estimated 300,000 horses working in London in the late 19th century, producing some 400-500 tons of manure daily. In the vicinity of hospitals, straw was spread on the streets in an effort to deaden the noise of the horses' feet and clattering carriage wheels.

A Clydesdale and a Belgian Draught relax in their summer paddock.

HORSE LOVERS

Anne, The Princess Royal
(b. 15 August, 1950)
Horses have always played an important part in the life of the English Princess Royal, who made history in 1971 as the first member of a royal family to become European Three-Day Event Champion. It was very much a family victory because the horse she rode, Doublet, was out of an Argentine polo pony mare called Sureté that her father, Prince Philip, had played for many years. The princess later became an accomplished amateur jockey, both on the flat and over fences, winning races on, among others, Insular, bred and owned by the Queen, and her own steeplechaser Cnoc-na-Cuille.

This exuberant stallion shows the grace, strength and perfect natural balance possessed by all horses.

~ *March* ~

~ 15 ~

MYTHOLOGICAL HORSES

According to Scandinavian legend, Hrimfaxi was the Horse of Night. It was from his bit that 'rime-drops' or dew fell on the earth.

WAR HORSES

Eighteenth-century troopers' horses were trained in much the same way as present-day police horses: La Traité sur la Cavalerie by Count Drummond de Melfort, published in 1784, shows men waving flags, beating drums and firing guns to accustom their mounts to the strange sights and sounds of the battlefields.

~ 16 ~

~ 17 ~

~ 18 ~

~ 19 ~

~ 20 ~

~ 21 ~

An Arabian adopting the breathtaking elevated trot for which the breed is famed.

~ 22 ~

~ 23 ~

HORSE DOCTORS

A ride on a piebald horse was said to cure a child of whooping cough; a few hairs from a stallion's tail, twisted into a necklace, were reputed to cure the wearer of goitre.

~ 24 ~

~ 25 ~

~ 26 ~

~ 27 ~

~ 28 ~

HORSE HEROINES

La Pie

La Pie was the name of a most unusual mount for a Marshal of France. Not only was she a mare, she was also piebald. Despite her sex and colour, she was the favourite horse of Henri de la Tour d'Auvergne, Viscount of Turenne, and he was astride her, ahead of his army, when he was mortally wounded on July 27, 1675, towards the end of the Dutch War. It was almost impossible to fall out of the type of saddle used at that time, and when the Marshal was shot he remained aboard La Pie. The mare halted, hesitated for a brief moment, then turned and took her master back to his fellow officers. Bereft of their commander, the French troops faltered, wondering what their next move should be. Then a voice shouted 'Turn the mare loose, she will show us the way to victory.' One version of the story claims she was indeed turned loose, another suggests she had an officer at her head. Either way, the brave piebald mare began her customary unhurried march towards the enemy army, leading the French troops boldly into battle. She survived the war, spending her retirement contentedly on the lands of a French monastery.

The paint horse has good natural camouflage.

Tradition holds that brown and white horses are unlucky. It is hard to believe that of this fine skewbald.

~ 29 ~

~ 30 ~

~ 31 ~

HORSE LOVERS

Queen Anne
*(b. February 6, 1665,
d. August 1, 1714)*
*When not occupied with affairs of
state, Queen Anne derived great
enjoyment from hunting and racing.
As a child she used to ride daily with
her father, James, Duke of York (later
James II). Later, when poor health
and increasing weight made riding
difficult, she followed hounds in a
carriage. According to Dean Swift,
writing in 1711, 'she hunts in a chaise
with one horse, which she drives like
Jehu…' She maintained a string of
racehorses at Newmarket, as well as
the Royal Stud at Hampton Court,
and inaugurated the first race meeting
at Ascot on August 11, 1711.*

HORSE LEAPS

*While out one day with the Quorn
foxhounds the hunter ridden by the
5th Earl of Lonsdale (1857-1944)
was reputed to have cleared, in one
leap, an obstacle comprising a set of
rails, a ditch and a second set of rails,
the distance from take-off to landing
measuring 32ft (9.85m).*

Some people consider four white socks a blessing. Others take quite the opposite view.

There is nothing more appealing than a bright-eyed foal.

~ *April* ~

Riding is a partnership. The horse lends you his strength,
speed and grace, which are greater than yours. For your part
you give him your guidance, intelligence and understanding, which
are greater than his. Together you can achieve
a richness that alone neither can.

RIDING *The True Techniques*

Lucy Rees

The courageous, energetic April horse makes an ideal mount for tough competitive sports.

~ April ~

~ 1 ~

Appaloosa mare and foal

~ 2 ~

~ 3 ~

HORSE FACTS

A 19th-century equestrian statue of the Duke of Wellington, by Matthew Coates Wyatt, stood 10 metres high. It took three years just to make the plaster cast and when it was cast in bronze a dinner party for 12 people was held in the horse's belly.

~ 4 ~

~ 5 ~

~ 6 ~

~ 7 ~

HORSE LOVERS

John Skeaping
(1901-1980)

The British sculptor and painter John Skeaping enjoyed a worldwide reputation as a leading sculptor and draughtsman of horses. He developed an early love of draught horses and was devastated when, at the outbreak of the Great War, he saw them being requisitioned by the Army. Later he learned to race-ride and, when injury eventually put a stop to that, he went show jumping. He once had an eerie experience when working on a bronze of Paul Mellon's Derby winner, Mill Reef. One morning, removing the wet cloths used to keep the clay model moist, he found that the clay had slipped from one of the horse's forelegs, exposing the supporting framework. Shortly afterwards he learned that Mill Reef had broken that same leg in a training gallop that very morning.

In the USA a horse with a spotted coat is called an Appaloosa. The name is a corruption of the Palouse river.

IMPERIAL HORSES

Incitatus (meaning 'spurred on') was the favourite racehorse of the Roman Emperor Gaius Caesar (AD12-41), known as Caligula. The stallion was originally called Porcellus ('little pig') but Caligula changed his name when he began to win races. Eventually the Emperor became so obsessed with the horse that he made him a citizen of Rome and proposed that he should be elected consul. Incitatus was provided with a marble stable, a manger carved from ivory, a gold bucket, purple trappings and a jewelled collar.

~ 8 ~

~ 9 ~

~ 10 ~

~ 11 ~

~ 12 ~

~ 13 ~

~ 14 ~

A 'drinker of the wind'

HORSE LOVERS

Peter O'Sullivan
(b. March 3, 1918)
Peter O'Sullivan, British racing journalist and doyen of sports commentators, has had a lifelong affinity with horses. Ever since the age of seven, when he rode (illegally) his pony Fairy around Epsom racecourse, his work and leisure have been inextricably linked with horses and racing. He has owned a number of successful racehorses, including the sprinter Be Friendly and Attivo, a spirited little horse with the heart of a lion who won on the Flat and over hurdles. On more than one occasion Peter has found himself undertaking the nerve-racking task of calling home his own winners live on television. Escaping from the commentary box in time to accompany his horse into the winner's enclosure has not always been easy!

Horses have a natural suspicion of water, but this stallion seems happy to paddle in a shallow stream.

~ 15 ~

~ 16 ~

~ 17 ~

~ 18 ~

~ 19 ~

POST HORSES

In 16th-century France, King Henry IV established a postmaster in every town of any size, with relays of horses to be ridden by postboys. Each post horse was marked on the right quarter with an 'H' beneath a crown, and on the left with the initial letter of its town. Because horses were in short supply after the civil wars, it was forbidden to gallop a post horse, offenders being subject to a fine.

HORSESHOES

The patron saint of blacksmiths is St Eloi, who appears to have had an unusual method of shoeing restive horses. If certain sculptures of him are to be believed, he simply cut off the horse's leg, affixed the shoe to the hoof and then replaced the limb!

~ 20 ~

~ 21 ~

All horses love to roll.

A meadow full of nutritious grass is an ideal environment for a growing foal.

~ 22 ~

~ 23 ~

~ 24 ~

~ 25 ~

~ 26 ~

~ 27 ~

~ 28 ~

Foals often seem to have a limitless supply of energy.

PERSONALITY HORSES

Eclipse
(b. April 1, 1764 - d. February 26, 1789)

The unbeaten thoroughbred Eclipse is widely regarded as one of the greatest racehorses of all time, renowned for his ground-devouring stride, his tremendous stamina and the ease with which he beat the finest horses in England. After Eclipse's death a professor at the Royal Veterinary College in London made a study of his remains to try to discover the secret of his success. His research revealed that the horse, who stood less that 16hh, could cover 25ft with each stride. He also found that Eclipse's heart weighed 14lbs, some 5lbs more than the average adult horse's heart.

PSYCHIC HORSES

Newmarket racecourse is said to be haunted by the ghost of the jockey Fred Archer, who was born in 1857 and shot himself at the age of 29. Instances have been recorded of horses slowing down, or swerving at precisely the same spot on the track for no clear reason. Spectators and jockeys saw two such incidents in 1949 and 1950 and reported something white and spectral hovering over the racing horses.

Despite domestication, horses remain at heart herd animals and are never happier than when at liberty together.

~ April ~

HORSE LORE

There was an old belief that the skulls of horses were endowed with the ability to enhance sound. In the 17th century during restoration work on the church of St Cuthbert at Elsdon, Northumberland, three horses' skulls were found in the stone spirelet of the bell-cote, placed there, it is said, as acoustic devices. The skulls of horses were also laid under the floor of a house in the belief that they would improve the tone of a piano that stood above them.

~ 29 ~

~ 30 ~

Ever careful of his feet, this foal drinks gingerly alongside his dam.

OPERATIC HORSES

The Swedish soprano Birgit Nilsson (b. May 17, 1918), famed for her performances of the great Wagnerian roles, is also noted for her broad sense of humour and it became a tradition to play jokes on her in the studio during recording sessions. When she was singing the part of Brünnhilde in the first-ever complete recording of Wagner's Ring cycle her colleagues planned a particularly elaborate joke. At the moment towards the end of Götterdämmerung when Brünnhilde calls for her faithful steed Grane to carry her into the flames of Siegfried's funeral pyre, the wing doors of the stage suddenly opened and in came a real live horse. Nilsson is reported to have almost fallen over with surprise and recording stopped while the Vienna Philharmonic Orchestra burst into cheers. The horse, having been previously rehearsed so as not to be scared of the huge orchestral forces, played his part to perfection!

Young foals gain confidence by staying close to their dams, who are very protective of them when they are young.

~ *May* ~

'Hast thou given the horse strength? Hast thou clothed his neck with thunder? …. He paweth in the valley, and rejoiceth in his strength: he goeth on to meet the armed men. He mocketh at fear, and is not affrighted; neither turneth he back from the sword. The quiver rattleth against him, the glittering spear and the shield. He swalloweth the ground with fierceness and rage … He saith among the trumpets, Ha, ha: and he smelleth the battle afar off, the thunder of the captains, and the shouting.'

The Book of Job, Chapter 39

The May horse can be obstinate, but is usually dependable and courageous.

~ 1 ~

The aristocratic Paso from Peru.

~ 2 ~

~ 3 ~

HERBAL HORSES

Fennel is one of the world's oldest cultivated plants. The Romans ate it for its health-giving properties, the ladies believing that it prevented obesity. It was held sacred by the Anglo-Saxons for its power against evil. Tradition has it that a horse that is difficult to catch will be unable to resist fennel-flavoured gingerbread.

~ 4 ~

HORSE FACTS

When horses, designed by nature to live in rolling open grassland, are kept in confined spaces, with insufficient exercise, they are liable to develop stable 'vices', a somewhat harsh term for habits acquired through boredom. Some are called 'weavers' – they rock continually from one side to another. Others 'crib-bite', that is they grip any available object, such as the door or manger, with their teeth and take in gulps of air. Others, who swallow air without actually biting anything, are termed 'wind-suckers'. Turning horses out to grass for a few hours each day is the best preventative.

~ 5 ~

~ 6 ~

~ 7 ~

This herd from the Tersk Stud enjoys a near-natural life in the rolling grasslands of Russia's Northern Caucasus.

~ May ~

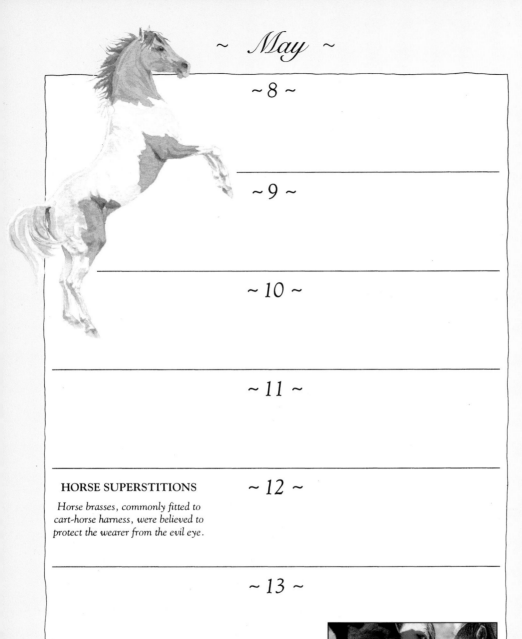

~ 8 ~

_____

~ 9 ~

_____

~ 10 ~

_____

~ 11 ~

_____

HORSE SUPERSTITIONS

Horse brasses, commonly fitted to cart-horse harness, were believed to protect the wearer from the evil eye.

~ 12 ~

_____

~ 13 ~

_____

~ 14 ~

Me for the mineral lick!

HORSE HEROES

Sefton and Copenhagen

On Tuesday, July 20, 1982, 16 men and horses of the Household Cavalry Mounted Regiment set off on a routine journey from their Knightsbridge Barracks in London to take up guard duty in Whitehall. As they passed unsuspectingly through Hyde Park a bomb, placed in a parked car, exploded. Four men were fatally injured and one horse was killed outright. Six others were so badly injured that they had to be shot on the spot. Of the survivors two horses in particular caught the public imagination: Sefton and Copenhagen. Sefton was 19, the oldest horse on duty that day. A piece of flying metal had pierced his jugular vein, which was bleeding so profusely that a soldier removed his shirt and stuffed it into the wound to try to stem the flow. The 11-year-old Copenhagen had multiple injuries, including a severed saliva duct and nails and pieces of shrapnel embedded in deep wounds in his knees and face.

That both horses survived is a tribute to the skill of the veterinary surgeons who tended them, removing literally dozens of pieces of shrapnel and nails from their battered bodies, and to the indomitable courage of the two horses themselves. Both eventually returned to duty, Sefton for a couple of years, Copenhagen for nearly seven years. After retirement, Sefton went to the Home of Rest for Horses in Buckinghamshire and Copenhagen to the International League for the Protection of Horses in Norfolk. After the bombing Copenhagen lost the proper use of his vocal chords and when he tried to whinny he could only grunt. That, coupled with less than perfect manners in the stable, earned him the affectionate nickname, 'The Pig'.

Horses in their natural state graze for up to twenty hours out of every twenty-four.

~ *May* ~

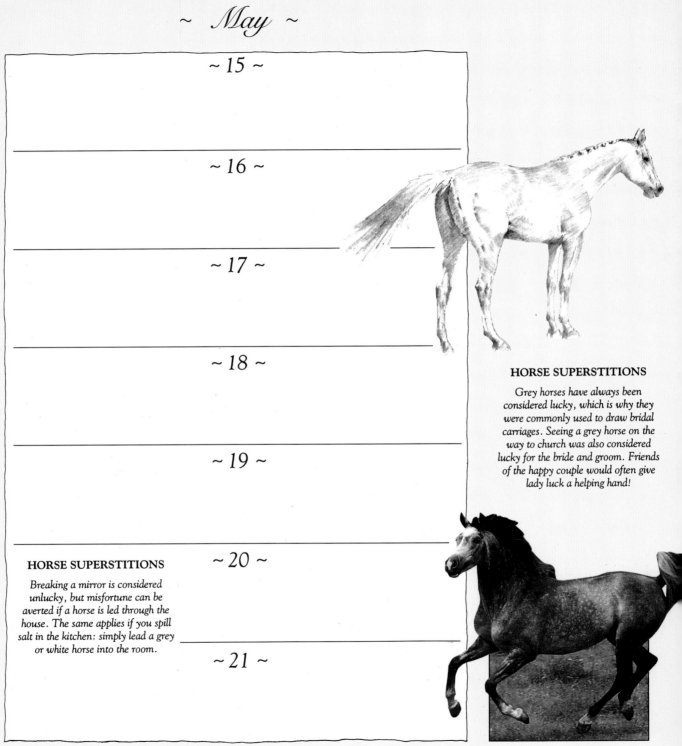

~ 15 ~

~ 16 ~

~ 17 ~

~ 18 ~

~ 19 ~

HORSE SUPERSTITIONS

Grey horses have always been considered lucky, which is why they were commonly used to draw bridal carriages. Seeing a grey horse on the way to church was also considered lucky for the bride and groom. Friends of the happy couple would often give lady luck a helping hand!

~ 20 ~

HORSE SUPERSTITIONS

Breaking a mirror is considered unlucky, but misfortune can be averted if a horse is led through the house. The same applies if you spill salt in the kitchen: simply lead a grey or white horse into the room.

~ 21 ~

Grey horses are considered lucky.

The finely chiselled features of the Arabian have captured the hearts of countless admirers of horses.

~ May ~

~ 22 ~

HORSE SUPERSTITIONS

Riding whips were often made of wood from the rowan tree, a well-known safeguard against witchcraft. Carrying a rowan-wood whip was supposed to prevent witches from casting a spell on a horse.

~ 23 ~

~ 24 ~

HORSE FACTS

'Galvayne's Groove' is a brown mark that appears on the corner incisor teeth of a horse, extending down the tooth as the horse grows older and making it possible to estimate the animal's age. It takes its name from Sydney Galvayne, an Australian horse trainer of the late 19th century. Some doubt exists as to whether he was in fact the first man to appreciate the significance of the groove or whether it was the discovery of an American horse tamer called 'Professor' Sample. Either way, Galvayne, author of Horse Dentition, *among other works, was certainly responsible for bringing it to the attention of horsemen.*

~ 25 ~

~ 26 ~

~ 27 ~

~ 28 ~

The Australian pony resembles the Welsh breeds from which it is descended.

HORSE TAILS

The tail of the Exmoor pony fans out at the top and is known as an 'ice' tail because it gives protection from severe weather. The Exmoor is Britain's oldest breed of native pony and one of the oldest of all equine breeds, having existed on the moors since before the Ice Age.

~ 29 ~

~ 30 ~

~ 31 ~

The Welsh pony combines striking good looks with great hardiness.

HORSE HEROES
Ben

There are many stories about pit ponies saving the lives of the coal miners with whom they worked. One concerned a pony called Ben, who normally shared his driver's lunchtime sandwiches. One day Ben refused to join in the meal, standing instead a little distance away and pawing the ground with his foot. At first the driver ignored him, but when Ben began to become more restless and started to whinny and then back away, he decided to follow the pony. Almost immediately the roof collapsed at the very spot where he had been sitting.

Scratching one's nose is easy with legs as long as these.

~ *June* ~

What do we, as a nation, care about books?
How much do you think we spend altogether on our libraries, public or
private, as compared with what we spend on our horses?

Of Kings' Treasuries
John Ruskin (1819-1900)

June's foal is full of nervous energy: even when he is at rest, his senses are keenly alert.

~ June ~

~ 1 ~

HORSE DOCTORS

The 3rd-century bishop, writer and martyr St Hippolytus was also a noted horse doctor. It is said that after his bones were buried beneath the altar of a church in Herefordshire people with injured or sick horses would take them, via the north door of the church, to the altar, where they would be touched by the saint's relics in return for an offering of thanks.

~ 2 ~

~ 3 ~

~ 4 ~

~ 5 ~

~ 6 ~

~ 7 ~

A Clydesdale foal amid daisies

HORSE LEAPS

A place called Bayard's Leap in Lincolnshire is said to be the scene of prodigious leaps by a mare name Bayard. Urged on by both her rider and a witch, who was also perched on her back, she is reputed to have cleared a distance of 300ft in four bounds – after which she died.

HORSE LORE

In parts of Britain there was an ancient belief that possession of a toad's bone endowed a person with power over horses. The bone, it was said, must come from a toad whose flesh has been devoured by ants. The skeleton is thrown into a fast-flowing stream and the bone that becomes detached from the rest and floats upstream, screaming (!), will make its possessor a toadman with control over horses.

The Clydesdale, Scotland's heavy horse breed, is noted for its spirited action which belies its large proportions.

~ June ~

LITERARY HORSES

The Maltese Cat is the most famous polo pony in fiction, a flea-bitten grey, brilliantly quick on his feet, who knows more about 'playing the game' than most humans. He is the creation of Rudyard Kipling (1865-1936)

~ 8 ~

~ 9 ~

~ 10 ~

WAR HORSES

When the Royal Scots Greys regiment was sent to the Boer War in 1899 it soon became apparent to the men that their greys were dangerously conspicuous against the South African terrain. Their solution was to dye their horses' coats with sodium permanganate, which resulted in the greys becoming 'chestnuts' for several weeks at a time!

~ 11 ~

HORSESHOES

The luckiest horseshoes are said to be those found by accident, for instance in the road. Especially propitious is a shoe cast from the near hindleg of a grey mare.

~ 12 ~

~ 13 ~

~ 14 ~

Designed for speed, the horse has long legs, big hindquarters (his 'engine') and a deep girth providing ample room for his heart and lungs.

~ June ~

~ 15 ~

~ 16 ~

RECORD-BREAKING HORSES

The oldest recorded age for a pony is believed to be 54, achieved by a French farmer's stallion, born in 1919.

~ 17 ~

~ 18 ~

LITERARY HORSES

In The Adventures of Don Quixote of La Mancha by Miguel Cervantes (1547-1616) the hero deliberates for four days before devising the name Rozinante (from rosin, a common drudge horse, and ante, before) for his horse. In Quixote's eyes this broken-down animal, all skin and bone, is superior to Alexander's Bucephalus or the Cid's Babieca: 'He finally determined upon Rosinante, importing that he had only been a rozin, a drudge-horse, before his present condition, and that now he was before all the rozins in the world.'

~ 19 ~

~ 20 ~

~ 21 ~

A warmblood foal. Originally bred to pull carriages, warmbloods have been refined with Thoroughbred blood for riding purposes.

~ *June* ~

A foal needs good pasture if he is to thrive and grow.

HORSE FACTS

The 'dancing white horses' of Vienna's world famous Spanish Riding School are born black or brown and only turn grey as they grow older.

~ 22 ~

~ 23 ~

~ 24 ~

~ 25 ~

~ 26 ~

~ 27 ~

~ 28 ~

HORSE HEROES

Foxhunter

Foxhunter was the best horse ever ridden by Lt Colonel Sir Harry Llewellyn, one of Britain's leading show jumping riders in the 1940s and 1950s. The pair became national heroes when they helped the British team win the Olympic gold medal in 1952, their country's only victory in any sport at the Helsinki Olympic Games. When Foxhunter died, Sir Harry buried his heart in the hills near his Abergavenny home. An inscribed tablet set in the rock nearby commemorates this great athlete.

PERSONALITY HORSES

Cornishman V

One of the stars of the film of Dick Francis' book Dead Cert was the famous three-day event horse Cornishman V, Olympic team gold medal winner in 1968 and World Champion in 1970. During one exciting action sequence in the film Cornishman was required to jump over the bonnet of a taxi, a 'stunt' he performed with great élan, ears pricked at the camera!

The fleabitten appearance of this mare is the result of brown specks of hair on an otherwise grey coat.

~ 29 ~

~ 30 ~

HORSE LEAPS

The Major's Leap in Shropshire commemorates a feat achieved by a Major Thomas Smallman during the 17th century. To escape pursuit by the Roundheads, the Major jumped his horse from the crest of Wenlock Edge, landing in a tree below. The horse was killed, but his fortunate rider survived.

The powerfully built Andulucian

RECORD-BREAKING HORSES

The official high-jump record for a horse is 2.47m (8ft, 1¼ in), set in Santiago, Chile, in 1949 by a 15-year-old failed racehorse called Huaso. The rider was Captain Alberto Larraguibel Morales. Several horses are known to have jumped greater heights before official records were kept. In the USA Heatherbloom, ridden by Dick Donnelly, cleared 2.515m (8ft, 3in) at a public demonstration in 1902.

Spain's elegant Andalucian is a horse of ancient origins noted for his proud action and docile temperament.

~ *July* ~

'A proof that the horse enjoys running is that when he has got loose he never moves at a walk, but runs. It is his nature to enjoy it, unless he is obliged to run an excessive distance. Neither horse nor man likes anything in the world that is excessive.'

The Art of Horsemanship
Xenophon (430 -350 BC)

July's horse, with her loving and protective nature, makes the ideal broodmare.

~ 1 ~

~ 2 ~

~ 3 ~

~ 4 ~

~ 5 ~

~ 6 ~

~ 7 ~

HORSE FIGHTS

In Iceland and also in Norway, horse fights used to be a popular form of entertainment. Two stallions, who would fight naturally in the wild for possession of a mare, would be trained and set against each other to amuse the public and also, doubtless, to prove which was best for breeding purposes. Handlers used goads to urge the stallions to bite and kick and strike out at each other. Not infrequently at these fights the attendants were injured or even killed.

Colts often indulge in play fights.

Wide-set eyes give a horse a generous appearance, as well as an extensive field of vision, enabling him to spot approaching dangers.

HORSE LORE

There was an old belief that a person wishing to put a curse on an enemy should set a horse's head on a pole, the muzzle pointing in his or her direction and the mouth propped open with a stick.

~ 8 ~

~ 9 ~

HISTORICAL HORSES

When Smerdis, King of Persia, died in 522 BC those vying to succeed him agreed that the throne should go to the owner of the horse which neighed first when they met the next day. Darius's clever groom showed his charge – a stallion – an in-season mare at the designated place so that when the horse was taken to the same spot the following day he immediately began to neigh in the hope that she would reappear, thereby innocently winning the throne for his master.

~ 10 ~

~ 11 ~

~ 12 ~

~ 13 ~

This Saddlebred foal already shows the fire and speed typical of the breed.

~ 14 ~

Reassured by the proximity of his dam, the young foal peers inquisitively about him to learn about the world.

~ 15 ~

~ 16 ~

~ 17 ~

HORSE LAUGHS

At the coronation of George III, Lord Talbot, the Lord High Steward, was required to ride into Westminster Hall and up to the throne, swear allegiance to the king and ride out again. Talbot had gone to some trouble to school his horse so that he could back respectfully out of the king's presence. Unfortunately on the big day the horse quite mistook his master's commands and insisted on approaching the throne rump-first – causing a great deal of mirth to the assembled throng.

~ 18 ~

~ 19 ~

RECORD-BREAKING HORSES

The tallest living horse in the world is said to be a Shire gelding named Bovington Black King. Born in 1984 at the National Shire Horse Centre in Devon, England, he stands 19.2hh (1.98m).

~ 20 ~

~ 21 ~

The Shire descends from England's war horse and is considered by many to be the supreme heavy breed.

~ *July* ~

HORSE FACTS

When the North American Indians first set eyes on the horses reintroduced into the continent by the conquistador Cortés, they called them 'big dogs'. Horses had been extinct on the North American continent for many thousands of years and there was, accordingly, no word in the language of the native people to describe them.

~ 22 ~

~ 23 ~

~ 24 ~

~ 25 ~

~ 26 ~

~ 27 ~

~ 28 ~

The striking-looking Pinto

HORSE HEROES
Comanche

In 1868 Captain Myles Keogh, serving with the 7th Cavalry at Fort Leavenworth, Kansas, chose a new charger from a draft of 40 remounts. The 15hh buckskin (yellow dun) gelding was six years old and cost him $90. He proved to be a comfortable ride, with endless stamina and a good temperament.

Soon afterwards, during a skirmish against the Comanche Indians at Bluff Creek, the gelding was injured by an arrow in his quarters, yet nevertheless patiently carried his rider out of the fray and showed great fortitude when the steel arrow was later extracted. Keogh named him Comanche.

On June 25, 1876, Keogh on Comanche found himself riding with General Custer's detachment into the most devastating defeat ever suffered by the US forces at the hands of the North American Indians. 'Custer's Last Stand' claimed the lives of Custer and all of the 200 troops with him. When General Terry's relief force arrived the next day, they found one horse still alive: Comanche. Flies were swarming over a dozen bloody wounds and several arrow shafts projected from his neck and quarters. Against all odds he survived the 950-mile journey to the regimental headquarters and recovered to parade on ceremonial occasions, saddled but riderless. He died at the age of 29 and his body was put on permanent display in Kansas University museum.

These Overo-type Pintos have a solid coat colour with splashes of white. Blue eyes are not uncommon in Pintos.

~ *July* ~

~ 29 ~

PHANTOM HORSES

A big black horse ridden by the Duke of Monmouth is said to appear near the scene of the Battle of Sedgemoor each year on the anniversary of the battle. The horse carries his master away at speed, but his galloping hooves make no sound.

~ 30 ~

~ 31 ~

LITERARY HORSES

Right Royal is the equine hero of John Masefield's epic steeplechasing poem of that name which traces the hopes, disappointments, near disasters, despair and ultimate triumph of the 'big dark bay with the restless tread' and his young rider, Charles Cothill. Charles, having dreamt he has won the English 'Chasers' Cup, has wagered all he possesses on this one race. In the dying strides of the race the courageous Right Royal gets up to win by half a length. But Charles' fortune has not been made: the bookie who took his wager never pays up.

The air of heaven is that which blows between a horse's ears – Arabian saying

Horses often rear in play or when they are startled or excited.

~ *August* ~

You can't have perfect horses any more than you can perfect men, or perfect women. You put up with red hair, or bad teeth, or big feet, – or sometimes with the devil of a voice. But a man when he wants a horse won't put up with anything! Therefore those who've got horses to sell must lie.'

Can You Forgive Her?
Anthony Trollope (1815-82)

The horse born in August exudes self-confidence.

~ August ~

~ 1 ~

~ 2 ~

~ 3 ~

~ 4 ~

~ 5 ~

~ 6 ~

~ 7 ~

The tail: nature's flywhisk

HORSE LORE

When a foal is born it has in its mouth a substance known as the milt, similar in appearance to a small piece of liver and believed to prevent fluid entering the lungs before and during birth. It disappears rapidly after birth, but old horsemen who were fast enough to retrieve it believed that by drying the milt and keeping it in their clothing they would be imbued with magical powers over horses.

MYTHOLOGICAL HORSES

Epona, a name meaning 'The Great Mare', was one of the few goddesses to be worshipped by the Celts both in Britain and on the Continent. The earliest known representation of her is on a water-pot, found in England's New Forest and dating from around 100 BC. A slightly later bronze representation shows her seated on a throne, her hands resting on the heads of two foals. She was believed to preside over the mating of mares and the birth of foals: the word pony probably derives from her name.

Horses and ponies at grass appreciate shelter from the elements. A tall tree makes the perfect sunshade.

~ 8 ~

~ 9 ~

~ 10 ~

~ 11 ~

~ 12 ~

~ 13 ~

~ 14 ~

HORSE FACTS

The knight's warhorse of the Middle Ages had to be capable of carrying up to 900lbs in weight. That included the rider, the rider's arms and armour, his saddle and bridle and the horse's own armour.

HORSE HEROES

Marengo

Marengo was one of the favourite chargers of Napoleon Bonaparte. Standing only 14.1hh, he was a grey Arabian stallion imported from Egypt as a six-year-old in 1799 after the Battle of Aboukir. He took his name from the Battle of Marengo, during which the Emperor, wounded when a cannon shot hit his boot, was greatly impressed with the little horse's speed and courage under fire. Marengo carried Napoleon at Austerlitz, Jena, Wagram, and, finally, at Waterloo. During the latter Marengo was said to have received a minor wound in his left hip, the eighth time he had been wounded in action. He was eventually bought by General Angerstein of the Grenadier Guards and ended his days in England, living to the ripe old age of 38.

You can lead a horse to water ...

A contented Arabian mare poses for the camera with her well-grown youngster.

~ 15 ~

HORSE BREEDS
The Missouri Fox Trotter

The Missouri Fox Trotter is a North American breed, named for its exceptionally smooth paces. It was developed by early settlers who needed a comfortable, sure-footed riding horse with considerable stamina. The fox trot is a 'broken' gait in which the horse walks with his front legs and trots behind, sliding his feet under him as he goes, instead of striking them down hard, as in the normal trot. The Fox Trotter can maintain this gait for long periods with minimal fatigue to himself and his rider.

~ 16 ~

~ 17 ~

~ 18 ~

RECORD-BREAKING HORSES

The world's smallest horse is the Argentinian Falabella, named after the family which developed it. Examples of the Falabella, a breed which has the characteristics of a miniature horse rather than those of a pony, have stood as small as 14-15in (35.5-38cm).

~ 19 ~

~ 20 ~

~ 21 ~

A long, thick mane protects the neck from the weather, while the forelock helps to keep flies from the eyes.

~ 22 ~

~ 23 ~

~ 24 ~

~ 25 ~

PSYCHIC HORSES

The well developed sixth sense possessed by horses was memorably demonstrated during the Second World War by a police horse called Ubique. Out on patrol one day, his rider P.C. Salmon turned from a side road, intending to proceed down the adjoining main road. Yet Ubique resolutely refused to budge. Seconds later, a flying bomb came down in the road exactly where the pair would have been if Ubique had obeyed his rider.

~ 26 ~

~ 27 ~

~ 28 ~

POST HORSES

Horses of all kinds have always been a popular subject for postage stamps. Often they feature as old-fashioned post horses or in paintings and statuary of or by the famous. Horse sports are also frequently depicted and occasionally the subject is a real horse.

Australia has commemorated outstanding racehorses such as Phar Lap and Tulloch; the Dominican Republic honoured the 1956 Olympic show jumping gold medallists Hans-Günter Winkler and Halla; Ireland paid tribute to another famous show jumper, Boomerang, and New Zealand depicted the famous harness racehorse, Cardigan Bay.

Summer high spirits

The refined head of the Australian pony gives testimony to the Arab influence in its Welsh forebears.

HORSE LEGENDS

The Prophet's Thumbmark, a small indentation and a whorl of hair resembling a thumbprint, is found on the necks of some horses, especially Arabians. It is said to date from the time when the Prophet Mohammed, at the end of a long journey through the desert, had all his horses released to drink. To test their obedience, as they approached the much-needed water, he called them back. Only five obeyed and these he blessed by placing his thumb on their necks. They are said to have founded the five best strains of Arabian horses.

~ 29 ~

~ 30 ~

~ 31 ~

HORSE LOVERS

Josephine Barstow
*(b. September 27, 1940)
The British soprano Josephine Barstow is famous internationally both for her singing and her fine dramatic gifts. She has appeared in many of the world's opera houses in roles as diverse as Richard Strauss' Salome, Janáček's Jenufa and the fearless Odabella, who in Verdi's Attila avenges her father's death by slaying the Hun. At home, away from the tormented lives of these stage heroines, she enjoys a much quieter pastime: breeding Arabian horses.*

This horse's ears are alert to sounds from all directions.

The mane (and tail) of the Arabian is exceptionally fine and silky.

~ *September* ~

Four things greater than all things are, –
Women and Horses, and Power and War.'

Ballad of the King's Jest
Rudyard Kipling (1865-1936)

September's horse is a discriminating individual.

~ September ~

~ 1 ~

~ 2 ~

~ 3 ~

~ 4 ~

RECORD-BREAKING HORSES

In 1929 66 horses started in the Grand National Steeplechase at Aintree. It is said to be the highest number of runners in one event in racing history. Only ten horses finished, the winner being the seven-year-old Gregalach. The biggest field for a flat race was 58, in the 1948 Lincolnshire Handicap, won by Commissar.

HORSE FACTS

The gestation period of the horse is approximately 340 days. A healthy foal is on its feet and drinking its mother's milk within two hours of birth.

~ 5 ~

~ 6 ~

~ 7 ~

The Welsh pony is sturdy and strong.

A foal is able to stand within a couple of hours of birth and quickly learns to co-ordinate its limbs.

~ September ~

~ 8 ~

~ 9 ~

~ 10 ~

~ 11 ~

~ 12 ~

~ 13 ~

~ 14 ~

LITERARY HORSES

Undoubtedly the best-known work of fiction featuring a horse is Black Beauty, which by 1939 was estimated to have sold some 20 million copies worldwide. It has been the subject of several feature films and has inspired numerous literary imitations. Its author, Anna Sewell (1820-78), wrote it after becoming an invalid following a childhood accident. For most of her adult life she relied on horses, either ridden or driven, in order to retain mobility. She was an ardent advocate of better treatment for them, especially the hard-worked harness horses, a theme which recurs throughout Black Beauty.

RECORD-BREAKING HORSES

The tallest horse on record was a Shire gelding named Sampson (later renamed Mammoth), bred in Bedfordshire and born in 1946. By 1950 he stood an incredible 21.2hh (2.19m).

An Andalucian stallion shows off.

Bay colouring – that is, a red-brown coat with black mane, tail and legs – is the predominant colour of many breeds.

~ September ~

~ 15 ~

HISTORICAL HORSES

Bucephalus (meaning bull-headed) was the famous black charger of Alexander the Great. When the horse died at the age of 30 Alexander, the only man who had been able to ride him, built the city of Bucephala as a mausoleum.

~ 16 ~

~ 17 ~

~ 18 ~

DEIFIED HORSES

A horse ridden by the conquistador Cortés in Honduras suffered an unusual fate at the hands of the natives. Cortés left El Morzillo ('the black') in the care of some friendly Indians after the horse went lame. Ignorant of even the basics of horse care, they fed him on choice fruits and meat, unaware that what he really needed was the grass that grew plentifully all around. Unwittingly, they seem to have starved him to death. Fearing Cortés' wrath, they built a stone image of the horse and worshipped it: El Morzillo became Tziunchau, the god of thunder and lightning.

~ 19 ~

~ 20 ~

~ 21 ~

Friends

The Percheron is a well-proportioned, free-moving heavy horse that originated in Normandy, France.

~ 22 ~

~ 23 ~

~ 24 ~

~ 25 ~

~ 26 ~

~ 27 ~

~ 28 ~

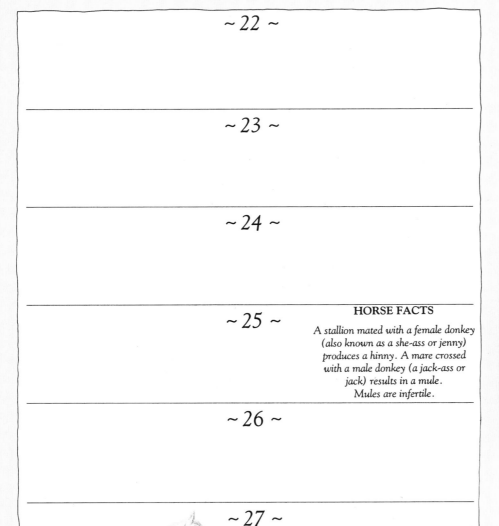

ERUDITE HORSES

Two Arab stallions, Muhammed and Zarif, and a Shetland pony named Hanschen were the star performers of the German horse trainer Karl Krall. Krall taught them to solve mathematical problems, including fractions and square and cube roots, to identify colours and scents and to recognise pictures. One expert suspected him of employing telepathy but changed his mind after working with Zarif in the absence of the trainer. Krall was emphatic that he simply used the same methods as those employed teaching a small child.

Grey horses have black skin.

HORSE FACTS

A stallion mated with a female donkey (also known as a she-ass or jenny) produces a hinny. A mare crossed with a male donkey (a jack-ass or jack) results in a mule. Mules are infertile.

HORSE SUPERSTITIONS

Walking beneath a ladder is said to bring bad luck, but this can be avoided if you subsequently keep your fingers crossed until you have seen three horses.

When at play, the tail – a valuable aid to balance as well as a fly-whisk – is often carried as a banner!

HERBAL HORSES

~ 29 ~

The herb elecampane used to be known as 'horse-heal' because it was believed to be a cure for mange.

~ 30 ~

PERSONALITY HORSES

Aldaniti

Bob Champion (b. June 4, 1948) was one of Britain's leading steeplechase jockeys when he was told, in July 1979, that he had cancer and that without treatment he would be dead in a matter of months. He survived a series of debilitating chemotherapy sessions and, determined to return to the sport he loved, fought his way back to fitness to ride in, and win, the 1981 Grand National. His partner on the great day at Aintree was an 11-year-old chestnut gelding called Aldaniti, in his own way just as heroic as his rider. Aldaniti was a class horse, but so injury-prone that he had managed to race only 16 times over fences. His most recent serious leg injury, sustained four months after Bob's cancer was diagnosed, had sidelined him for the whole of 1980. But fate decreed that on April 4, 1981, the 'two old crocks' should thrill the world by winning the most famous steeplechase of them all. The pair's achievements were later the subject of the film, Champions. In his retirement, Aldaniti has made many guest appearances to raise money for cancer relief.

An Arabian, released in his show bridle to show off for the camera.

Dark grey hairs on a grey base produce the attractive colouring known as dappled grey.

~ *October* ~

Round-hoofed, short-jointed, fetlocks shag and long,
Broad breast, full eye, small head and nostril wide,
High crest, short ears, straight legs, and passing strong,
Thin mane, thick tail, broad buttock, tender hide:
Look what a horse should have, he did not lack,
Save a proud rider on so proud a back.

Venus and Adonis
William Shakespeare (1564-1616)

October's horse is a friendly, sociable individual who makes a harmonious partner.

HORSE LEAPS

In 1733 Paulet St John is said to have jumped his horse safely across a yawning 25ft-deep chalk pit which he came upon unexpectedly while out riding. The horse subsequently became known as Beware Chalk Pit. A stone monument commemorates the feat at Farley Mount in Hampshire.

~ 1 ~

~ 2 ~

~ 3 ~

HORSE FACTS

With his long limbs and large heart and lungs, the horse is designed for galloping. Jumping is not a natural activity for horses and left to their own devices most will go round obstructions rather than over them. Careful training is required to accustom them to jumping. Even when they have been taught to jump, most horses will stay on the correct side of the paddock fence.

~ 4 ~

~ 5 ~

~ 6 ~

~ 7 ~

The eye-catching Fjord pony

Norway's Fjord pony is always dun in colour. It is tough, long-lived and a good worker, if a little wilful.

~ October ~

HORSE SUPERSTITIONS

According to tradition, to see a white horse is lucky. On doing so, it is customary to spit and make a wish, or to make a cross on the ground with your foot. You should keep your fingers crossed until you see a dog. The same ritual should be enacted on seeing a piebald (black and white) horse. To see a skewbald (brown and white) horse, however, is often considered unlucky.

~ 8 ~

~ 9 ~

~ 10 ~

~ 11 ~

~ 12 ~

~ 13 ~

~ 14 ~

Who's that?

ROYAL HORSES

Paddy

Paddy started his working life as a milk-cart horse on the streets of Edinburgh, until one day he was spotted by the Crown Equerry and taken to be shown to the Queen at Holyrood. With his skewbald markings and quiet disposition, he looked an ideal candidate for the role of drum horse with Her Majesty's Life Guards, so the Queen duly bought him. Paddy was moved to London, retrained and in due course, renamed. As Cicero he carried the regiment's drums on many ceremonial occasions.

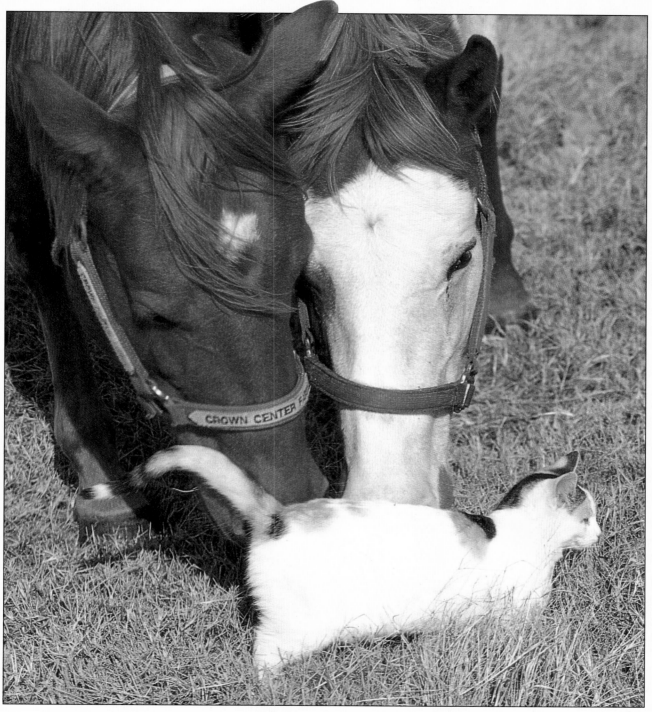

For all their size, horses are invariably gentle with smaller animals, making friends with cats especially.

~ 15 ~

~ 16 ~

~ 17 ~

ERUDITE HORSES

Lady Wonder, a mare owned by Mrs Claudia Fonda of Richmond, Virginia, was said to have correctly forecast the results of three Presidential elections and to have traced the body of a missing child. She could spell, do arithmetic and could even operate her own out-size typewriter.

RECORD-BREAKING HORSES

The official long-jump record for a horse is 8.40m (27ft, 6 ¾ in) set by Something, ridden by André Ferreira. in Johannesburg, South Africa, in 1975.

~ 18 ~

~ 19 ~

~ 20 ~

~ 21 ~

HORSE LOVERS

Princess Alia

Princess Alia, daughter of King Hussein of Jordan, takes an active part in the horse world, being both a rider and a breeder of Arabian horses. She is in charge of the Royal Jordanian Stud, which produces some beautiful examples of the breed. The Princess also takes a great interest in equine welfare. She has been known to rescue a sick or abandoned donkey on the roadside simply by putting it in the back of her car and taking it home with her!

Horses love – and need – freedom.

There are few places that cannot be reached by the teeth for a good scratch!

A handsome warmblood mare

~ 22 ~

~ 23 ~

~ 24 ~

HORSE LEAPS

A horse ridden by Thomas ap Harrie was reputed to have jumped clean over the standing stones known as Naid y March ('The Horse's Leap') in Wales. The distance between the stones, which range in height from 2ft, 6in (.6m) to 4ft (1.3m), is some 25ft (8m).

~ 25 ~

~ 26 ~

~ 27 ~

~ 28 ~

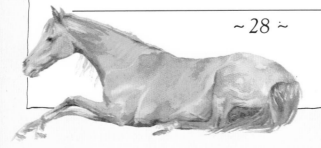

PERSONALITY HORSES

Combined Training

Major Geoffrey Brooke, a renowned British show jumping rider before and after the First World War, had two favourite horses, Alice and Combined Training, who were devoted stablemates. While on active service he rode the mare and the gelding alternately. On one occasion in France, Alice had to be left in the horse lines ten miles to the rear while Brooke rode Combined Training to the front. That evening the gelding refused to eat and became restive in his farm stable. During the night he disappeared: he had jumped over the lower half of the stable door and set off in search of his friend. He was later seen heading in the direction of enemy lines.

Amazingly, two days later he found his way back to the farm. Eventually he and Alice were reunited, greeting each other with neighs of delight. Alice was later wounded by splinters from a shell and sent back to England. Combined Training survived unscathed, but only just. As he was being ridden into action one day in March, 1918, he picked up a nail in his foot and Brooke had to change quickly to a troop horse. Not long afterwards several machine gun bullets hit the unfortunate troop horse and he had to be put down.

After the war Combined Training returned to show jumping. In 1921 he became the first British horse to win the coveted King George V Gold Cup at the International Horse Show in London and was a member of Britain's first winning Nations' Cup team. He lived to a ripe old age, spending his last years in retirement in Devon.

The horse's muzzle and whiskers are highly sensitive to touch, enabling him to assess objects he can't see clearly.

~ 29 ~

MYTHOLOGICAL HORSES

The Celts believed that after their death, their souls were carried on horseback to the land of the dead.

~ 30 ~

~ 31 ~

The Paso is a sturdy, short-legged riding horse.

HORSE LOVERS

Lillie Langtry
(b. October 18, 1852,
d. February 12, 1929)
The British actress Mrs Langtry, better known as 'The Jersey Lily', was one of the most beautiful and admired women of her day. She became a racehorse owner after being presented with a gift-horse, a two-year-old colt named Milford. Having registered as an owner under the pseudonym 'Mr Jersey', she began building up a string of horses. She enjoyed tremendous luck on the racecourse and was an enthusiastic gambler – when her horse Merman won the Cesarewitch in 1897 she collected £39,000, a fortune in those days.

Intelligence and kindness are the two main attributes of the Paso, in addition to his remarkably smooth paces.

~ *November* ~

'There's no secret so close as that between a rider and his horse.'

Mr Sponge's Sporting Tour
R.S. Surtees (1803-1864)

There is something undeniably magnetic about the mysterious November horse.

The honest head of a Przewalskii horse

~ 1 ~

~ 2 ~

~ 3 ~

HORSE BREEDS

The Asiatic Wild Horse

The most primitive horse breed known to survive to modern times is the Asiatic Wild Horse, also known as Przewalski's Horse, after the Polish colonel who discovered a wild herd in Mongolia in 1881. Many of the world's zoos keep these horses, some breeding them for proposed re-introduction into their wild Outer Mongolian homeland. The Asiatic Wild Horse has different characteristics from the domestic horse, including a higher chromosome count, and is always dun in colour with an upright mane.

~ 4 ~

~ 5 ~

~ 6 ~

~ 7 ~

Mutual grooming, performed here by two Przewalskiis (Asiatic wild horses), helps form relationships.

~ November ~

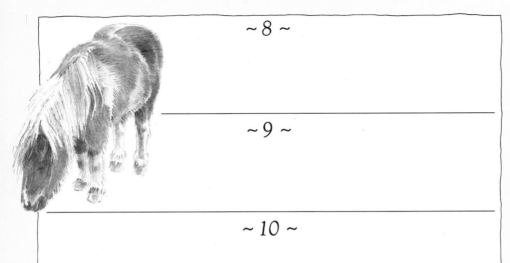

~ 8 ~

~ 9 ~

~ 10 ~

~ 11 ~

~ 12 ~

~ 13 ~

~ 14 ~

ERUDITE HORSES

In the 1590s a Scotsman named Banks toured the Continent with his celebrated horse Morocco, who, according to contemporary accounts, could count the numbers on a thrown dice, calculate the value of coins and correctly identify in the audience the owners of various items of property. Morocco's fame was such that Shakespeare mentions him in Love's Labour's Lost. Some say that Banks and his educated horse were eventually burned as witches.

A contented pair at grass

HORSE SUPERSTITIONS

In the west of Scotland if a horse neighs at the door of a house, it bodes sickness for the inhabitants.

Horses make friends by touching and smelling each other.

~ 15 ~

RECORD-BREAKING HORSES

The world speed record for a horse was set by the racehorse Big Racket in Mexico City on February 5, 1945. The four-year-old recorded 43.2 mph (69.62 km/h).

~ 16 ~

~ 17 ~

~ 18 ~

PERSONALITY HORSES

Warrior

The 1978 film International Velvet, made as a sequel to National Velvet (1944) and starring Nanette Newman, Tatum O'Neal, Anthony Hopkins and Christopher Plummer, recounts the story of a rebellious orphan who becomes a successful international rider. A number of well-known three-day event horses and riders were enlisted to do the serious action shots, among them British Olympic gold medallist Jane Holderness-Roddam. Jane and her great horse Warrior, winner of the tough Badminton and Burghley Horse Trials, doubled for Tatum O'Neal and Magic Lantern in the cross-country sequences. According to his rider, Warrior considered it the highlight of his career, revelling in the limelight and becoming thoroughly spoilt by all the attention!

~ 19 ~

~ 20 ~

~ 21 ~

There are five Appaloosa coat patterns: leopard, snowflake, blanket, marble and frost: these have leopard coats.

~ November ~

IMPERIAL HORSES

The Roman Emperor Hadrian was addicted to hunting. He named a town in Mysia 'Hadrianotherae' or Hadrian's hunting grounds. When his favourite hunter Borysthenes died, the Emperor had him buried there. The poem inscribed on the tomb extolling the horse's virtues is said to have been written by Hadrian himself.

HORSE ART

Horses were a constantly recurring image throughout the career of the French painter Eugène Delacroix (1798-1863). An entry in his Journal of April 15, 1823, when he was 25, reads: 'I must absolutely begin to draw horses. I must go to the stables every morning, go to bed very early, and get up very early.'

~ 22 ~

~ 23 ~

~ 24 ~

~ 25 ~

~ 26 ~

~ 27 ~

~ 28 ~

HORSE LORE

According to an old horseman's belief, if you experience difficulty controlling your horses, you should take their harness to a crossroads and recite from the Bible backwards, whereupon the Devil will appear, in the shape of a horse. Jump on his back and ride him, and you will have no more problems with your horses.

Leg bandages help prevent injury at play.

This exquisite head belongs to a Shagya Arabian, a strain produced in central and eastern Europe.

~ November ~

HORSE SUPERSTITIONS

~ 29 ~

According to tradition, the marrow of a horse, if boiled in wine, cooled, then warmed by the sun or by fire and used as an ointment is a cure for cramp.

~ 30 ~

Horses can survive severe weather provided they can find food.

HORSE HEROES

Mancha and Gata

Swiss-born traveller and writer Aimé Felix Tschiffely (1895-1954) proved conclusively the inherent stamina and endurance of the Criollo horse breed of the Argentine by riding from Buenos Aires to Washington D.C., in the United States. He set off in 1925, appropriately on April 23, St George's Day (the horse is an attribute of St George) with two Criollo horses, 16-year-old Mancha and 15-year-old Gata. Alternately riding one horse and leading the other as a pack horse, he completed the daunting journey in two-and-a-half years. The two horses were then shipped back to South America, where they spent their retirement on an estancia. Gate lived to be 36, Mancha died at the grand old age of 40.

A thick winter coat, with its accumulation of natural grease and dirt, helps give protection against the cold.

~ *December* ~

Where in this wide world can man find nobility without pride, friendship without envy or beauty without vanity? Here, where grace is laced with muscle, and strength by gentleness confined. He serves without servility; he has fought without enmity. There is nothing so powerful, nothing less violent; there is nothing so quick, nothing more patient. England's past has been borne on his back. All our history is his industry. We are his heirs, he our inheritance. Ladies and Gentlemen – the Horse!

Written for the Horse of the Year Show
Ronald Duncan (1954)

December's horse tends to be boisterous, full of fun, and ever so slightly clumsy!

~ 1 ~

ERUDITE HORSES

In 1906 a part-bred Arab mare called Princess Trixie, owned by American W. Harrison Barnes, was taken to London and for the following two years performed at the Palace Theatre where she astounded her audience with her ability to spell and do arithmetic, as well as to pick out colours. Trixie had been raised as a pet in the Barnes household and her owner had spent ten years training her by voice commands. Asked on one occasion to spell the word football, she selected the correct-sounding letters: FUTBAL. Barnes claimed she had the mental ability of a child of six and scientists and vets who carried out experiments with her could find no sign of tricks, such as signals from her owner.

~ 2 ~

~ 3 ~

~ 4 ~

~ 5 ~

~ 6 ~

~ 7 ~

HORSE SUPERSTITIONS

According to an old belief, if a horse drawing a hearse turned its head and neighed outside a house, there would soon be a death there.

Non-aggressive and designed to flee from danger, the horse is the epitome of strength, grace and speed.

LITERARY HORSES

In a satirical poem by Andrew Marvell (1621-1678), two horses, Charing and Woolchurch, grumble and gossip about the state of the nation under Stuart rule. The horses are London statues, left alone for the evening by their royal riders Charles I and Charles II (Charles I had gone to see Archbishop Laud, Charles II to visit a lady).

~ 8 ~

~ 9 ~

~ 10 ~

~ 11 ~

~ 12 ~

~ 13 ~

~ 14 ~

PSYCHIC HORSES

Horses are said to be psychic and capable of seeing ghosts. An encounter with a spirit invisible to a human being is likely to cause a horse to sweat and become restive. In the Middle Ages it was believed that horses were ridden by witches to their covens. Such 'hag-ridden' horses would be returned to their stables before dawn, dripping with sweat. A means of protection was to decorate a birch tree with white and red rags and prop it against the stable door on May Day.

Two youngsters make friends.

This warmblood evidently has a calm outlook on life.

~ December ~

~ 15 ~

HORSE FACTS

Such was its importance to the Bedouin of the Middle East that the Arabian horse appears in the holy book of Islam, the Koran, where the Prophet stresses the importance of preserving the breed's pure bloodlines, laying down specific rules as to how this should be achieved. Following these precepts, in Middle Eastern countries today a Moslem owner of a stallion will not charge a fee for his use, thereby enabling even poor owners of Arab mares to upgrade their stock.

~ 16 ~

~ 17 ~

~ 18 ~

~ 19 ~

~ 20 ~

~ 21 ~

HORSE BREEDS
The Arabian

The oldest pure breed of horse, the Arabian is said to have been fashioned by Allah from a handful of the south wind. Certainly it is physically different from other breeds, having 17 ribs, 5 lumbar bones and 16 tail vertebrae, whereas other horses have 18 ribs, 6 lumbar bones and 18 tail vertebrae. Developed in Arabia by nomadic Bedouin tribesmen, this beautiful animal lived in close proximity with its master, usually becoming 'part of the family' – a fact which accounts for its gentle nature and, perhaps, its sensitivity and intelligence.

WAR HORSES

The Arabian horse has long been the choice of endurance riders, since its stamina is second to none. This capacity for 'going forever' it owes to the Bedouin, who bred it to be the ultimate war horse, able to cover 100 miles at speed and fight a battle at the end of the journey. Its renowned agility was brought to the fore in such mounted sword fights between tribesmen, as during them its ability to 'turn on a sixpence' was of vital importance.

A reassuring word

Gypsy gold does not chink or glitter: it gleams in the sun and neighs in the dark – Irish gypsy saying

~ 22 ~

HORSE LEGENDS

Asbyrgi is a place in northern Iceland, a strange horseshoe-shaped gorge two miles long with rock walls towering 100 metres high all round. A narrow entrance at one end permits access to the sheltered ground between the cliffs which, if the visitor positions himself correctly, give a triple echo.

~ 23 ~

Geologists say Asbyrgi is a fault cliff situated in a zone of post-glacial volcanic activity. The Icelanders have a different explanation. One day the god Odin was galloping across the skies when his horse Sleipnir

~ 24 ~

stumbled. Putting down a foot to steady himself, he struck the northern tip of Iceland, leaving a huge hoof-shaped indentation. That is the spot that is now called Asbyrgi.

~ 25 ~

HORSE LEGENDS

In ancient Teutonic legend Saint Nicholas visited children on December 25 each year not in a sleigh drawn by reindeer but astride a white horse.

~ 26 ~

HORSESHOES

In folklore, iron was considered a strong defence against evil spirits, especially when shaped into a horseshoe. The latter is the symbol of the moon goddess and of fertility and was commonly nailed over a door to

~ 27 ~

bring good fortune to a household. Hung with the points downwards, it was believed to act as a charm against witchcraft. More recently it became usual to hang it the other way up to prevent the luck running out.

~ 28 ~

Waiting for the hay to arrive.

~ December ~

~ 29 ~

HORSE SENSE

The term 'stalking horse' is derived from the old ploy used by hunters of concealing themselves behind horses until they came within firing range of the game they were stalking.

~ 30 ~

~ 31 ~

Keeping up is sometimes hard work.

HORSE LOVERS

Elizabeth, Empress of Austria
(1837-1898)

Horses figured largely in the life of Elizabeth, Empress of Austria. A keen and gifted horsewoman, she played a major part in making riding to hounds popular with and acceptable for women. In 1876 she caused something of a sensation by spending six weeks in England, hunting in the Midlands. At her first opening meet she wore a close-fitting blue habit with gold buttons and wore her hair piled up under a top hat. She paid several more visits to Britain and Ireland to hunt, while at home she took a keen interest in her famous studs, both in Austria and Hungary, as well as undertaking high-school riding with her Lipizzaner Majestoso and training her well-known circus horses, Flick and Flock.

The Jutland, from Denmark, is a charming breed, combining strength with an exceptional willingness to please.

~ *Aquarius* ~

(January 21 – February 19)
The sign of the WATER BEARER

Tolerant, reserved, idealistic

The unpredictable nature of the horse born in Aquarius may be enough to put off many horse-lovers. Others will be disturbed by his strangely penetrating gaze, while still more will be affronted by his shrinking away from the friendly hand upon his pointy ear. But the world is as strange a place to the Aquarian horse as he is to it. It fascinates him, and so do you: just how do you bolt that door and why do you wear that odd-coloured jacket?

Intelligent and inventive, beware the equine escapologist (change the locks frequently just to be safe) for if there is one thing this horse dislikes it's having his freedom taken away. Democracy is very important to him too, so be prepared to negotiate, but also realise that he likes to be seen to be that little bit different: expect trouble if he has to wear the same old New Zealand rug that all the other horses sport and don't ask him to plod in line. His loathing of conformity and tendency to foot troubles make him an unlikely dressage competitor, while no Aquarian horse would be happy in a cavalry regiment or as a police horse. Content as one of the herd – albeit always a little way away from the rest – perhaps long-distance riding would be the most suitable occupation for this individual.

Compatible signs: *Libra and Gemini*

~ *Pisces* ~

(February 20 – March 20)
The sign of the FISH

Imaginative, peace-loving and kind

Typically smallish and graceful, the Piscean horse has large, liquid eyes and a dreamy, far-off expression. These are the horses favoured by greetings card companies and the inspiration for countless creations of soft-toy manufacturers (though they rarely come in blue or pink). Frequently, and with success, they are show ponies, with names like 'Sorrow's Silent Stream' or 'Spring is Closer Now'. Crowds gasp at their ethereal beauty, but don't clap too loud lest they appear gauche in the presence of this sensitive creature. Deeply imaginative, and therefore all too likely to see what isn't there, the Piscean pony is very likely to shy at nothing – learner riders be warned!

All is well when the Piscean horse is treated with reverence and kept from the harsh realities of life, but such is her delicate nature that she is ill-equipped to take criticism, make decisions (hay or neigh?) or cope when her owner forgets the mints. In such times of bitter sadness the fishy horse philosophically retreats into her own fantasy world and you will most likely not realise your thoughtlessness. Happiest as a doted-upon family pet, this horse will return the love it is given in plenty. Beware of hoof problems.

Compatible signs: *Cancer and Scorpio*

~ *Aries* ~

(March 21– April 20)
The sign of the RAM

New beginnings, energy, leadership

Horses born under the sign of the Ram are seldom a 'novice ride'. This sign rules the crushing of the groom against the stable door, the biting of the yard dog, rope burns, the knocking off of riders on overhanging branches, swearing blacksmiths and splintered woodwork. There will be times (every day) when you will curse him, but if you can handle him, he will be the best ride of your life.

Courageous, determined and wilful, Arian horses tremble with energy and have irrepressible, if simple, characters. Ideal as hunters, cross-country eventers, polo ponies or racehorses, the lean-framed Ram horses's tunnel vision will be invaluable, if a little frightening at times. These horses like to lead, to win and to celebrate in themselves. The Arian horse won't, therefore, be content pulling the rag-and-bone man's cart. Never put your young child on a ram-looking seaside donkey; at best they will be unable to speak for the rest of the day, at worst, you'll never see them again. Quite often a fiery chestnut colour, these horses are probably accountable for the reputation of the proverbial chestnut mare.

Compatible signs: *Leo and Sagittarius*

~ *Taurus* ~

(April 21 – May 21)
The sign of the BULL

Steadfast, courageous and firm

The Taurean horse is easily spotted: she is the one to whom all the children rush at the pony rides, hanging around her chubby neck, feeding her apples and rubbing their hands into her soft coat. She loves it, especially the apple part, she could take hours of that. As the sign of the Bull, these horses are often very broad-shouldered, muscular and solid. If you had a Taurean pony as a child you probably have bandy legs but lots of good memories.

The characteristics of a Taurean horse, her stoicism, dependability, compassion and good sense, make her an excellent first pony or truly unshakeable police horse. The original 'armchair ride', the horse ruled by Venus is typically a passive nag but beware of pushing your luck when she is being obstinate (most of the time) or she will let you know her displeasure in no uncertain terms – you've seen cowboys on bulls at the rodeo? Well, you get the picture. But keep her happy (this is where apples are so important) and all will be very well with this close-to-nature horse whose love of hearth and home is second to none. Beware of obesity and watch out for troubles with the back and throat.

Compatible signs: *Virgo and Capricorn*

~ Gemini ~

(May 22 – June 21)
The sign of the TWINS

Duality, versatility, the intellect

Riding a Gemini horse through a forest after sundown in autumn is not for the faint-hearted, for with every crack of dry wood beneath his hooves, every conker falling to the ground, every breath of wind in the leaves, he will leap out of his skin, before long leaving you either buried in the leaf mould with a long walk home, or just plain exhausted. Nervous energy runs like electricity through his veins, his mind is constantly alert, his eyes rolling, his teeth champing, and, oh yes, he neighs ceaselessly.

Gemini horses rarely sleep well and this may explain their jumpiness, if not make it more acceptable. It is the influence of Mercury that gives him these quicksilver characteristics, and also his apparent lack of warmth, though he is charming and very curious in a coltish sort of way. Since the Gemini horse is restless, like the Aquarian equine, be sure to check your security measures or you won't find him where you left him, for his mind is a formidable tool.
His competitive nature and lightning reflexes would stand him in good stead at Pony Club games, where he would excel at cutting corners. Watch for shoulder problems and broken wind.

Compatible signs: *Libra and Aquarius*

~ Cancer ~

(June 22 – July 23)
The sign of the CRAB

Sensitive, material and very romantic

A Cancerian horse makes the ideal brood mare – protective, loving and devoted, she will be content with the pastoral life, watching the clover grow and the foals getting fat and glossy. In the wild, however, these mares will defend the herd's youngsters with all the tenacity characteristic of the Crab, so when weaning take the necessary precautions for separating a half-ton shellfish from its young. (Or, more sensibly, get someone else to do it!)

Since she is a steady ride, given naturally to half-passing, watch out for your head as the Cancerian mare is wont to scurry sideways under overhanging branches or through doorways (they don't have to be open). These horses seek shelter like the Arian horse seeks action and they are often devoted to homes, defensive of territory and hate changes in surroundings. Ruled by the Moon, these horses are sensitive to lunar cycles and may be a bit moody, indulging in comfort-eating, laziness and general crabbiness. That said though, they nearly always have the manners of perfect ladies. Beware of excessive weight gain and colic, and keep the Crab horse happy with visits to the seaside.

Compatible signs: *Pisces and Scorpio*

~ Leo ~

(July 24 – August 23)
The sign of the LION

Self-confidence, enthusiasm, pride

Leo is the sign of the liberty horse, the flashy show jumper, the best in class. Impressive, proud and often blessed with remarkably glossy and luxuriant coat, he simply demands admiration. He is not usually all show, however, for there is great strength of character here (stubbornness) but vulnerability too (unavoidable considering that Leo horses have egos the size of polo pitches). Yet he is a warm, generous and benevolent King of Beasts, with a heart in proportion to his inflated ego.

Nice movers, these sun horses glide with all the carnivorous assurance of the lion, beating the ground with each footfall and glorifying in the sensation of their muscular shoulders shuddering with the impact and sending shock waves through their manes. (It's never a good idea to plait his mane, it will drive you both made and it looks much nicer wild and free.) Show jumpers who buck at the end of clear rounds are almost always Leos. You see, they might not seem to, but they do doubt themselves and they buck as if to say 'There, I always knew I could do it'. You, of course, never had any doubt in your brave steed, and often find yourself wishing he'd save his playfulness for the paddock.

~ Virgo ~

(August 24 – September 23)
The sign of the VIRGIN

Discriminative, methodical, logical

The Virgoan horse has a similar look in the eye to the Piscean, but she is not as much of a dreamer as she appears. Her little feet are firmly on the ground and her head full of steady, earthy thoughts, not dreams. The closest she gets to dreaming is wishing you would tidy up the yard. Mess upsets her, and whilst she will cause you less trouble that a more exuberant sign when it comes to washing rugs, her aversion to mud, wind and rain make her a poor prospect for hunting or cross-country. Nor is she keen on being one of the herd, preferring her own space and a large degree of autonomy. She is best suited, perhaps, to the fair-weather rider who stables her in a tidy, efficient livery yard. That said, though, she would probably shine at dressage, its precision and balance being welcome to her methodical nature.

Attention to diet is required, for the Virgoan horse is a fussy eater who may lose condition in the harder months, but don't worry too much over this because she is usually more robust than her slight frame suggests. However, it is important to worm regularly and supplement food with tasty tit-bits.

Compatible signs: Aries and Sagittarius

Compatible signs: Taurus and Capricorn

~ *Libra* ~

(September 24 – October 23)
The sign of the SCALES

Balance, justice, love of beauty

The Libran horse is friendly and sociable and exudes a peaceful presence into the busy yard. He is also more likely than most other nags to be waiting keenly for your arrival and to greet you with a whinny. It's not that he's terribly excited about exercising, but he does love to admire the changes in the landscape through the seasons, to glimpse the first snowdrop and smell the dawn. He is a romantic, you see, not an athlete, though he will try to do almost anything to please, so don't push him too hard, or his slender legs may break down.

In case of injury, there's nothing more therapeutic to the Libran horse than having luxury lavished upon him, clover hay, organic oats, a deep, shiny, golden straw bed topped up with kind words and affection do nicely. Don't let him lie too long in self-indulgence, though, as the scales of Libra are likely to tip towards hedonism or negative thinking. A stable with plenty of fresh air and a good view are important too. The wise Libran horse owner recognises that singing to their steeds and scratching their withers greatly improves performance and promotes a harmonious and rewarding partnership.

Compatible signs: *Gemini and Aquarius*

~ *Scorpio* ~

(October 24 – November 22)
The sign of the SCORPION

Tenacious, secretive, instensely psychic

The Scorpio horse is like those in a team of stunt horses which charge into the showground four-abreast. They are big, black, a bit sinister-looking, and you know that although the moustached man balancing in a standing position on them is grinning, really he is terrified. He has good reason to be if they are Scorpio horses, for the horse born under the influence of Pluto, the remotest planet, is, well … dangerous. Since Scorpio horses have an ego approaching the dimensions of the Leo's and all the volatile emotions of a broody rhino, many owners describe them as accidents waiting to happen – or ones that have.

Yet there is nevertheless something deeply magnetic about this sign and you may have bought her unwittingly. Perhaps you were captivated by her eyes, or maybe she just reminded you of a picture of a horse on the cover of a horror story you enjoyed as a child. On the plus side, however, she is loyal (though jealous), intense (though vengeful) and courageous (though strangely cautious with it). The reproduction system is governed by Scorpio, so beware unwanted 'Sons of Phantom'.

Compatible signs: *Cancer and Pisces*

~ Sagittarius ~

(November 23 – December 21)
The sign of the ARCHER

Extrovert, optimistic, independent

In an old hunting print you can spot the Sagittarian horse with ease: he is the big gangly bay, all hooves, fetlocks and knees, leaping well clear of the yawning ditch, his reins loose and his stirrups flying. He has what can only be described as a smile on his face and is paying no attention to the fact that, riderless, he is heading for the ground at top speed. His jockey can be seen on his knees a little way off, his hard hat pushed impossibly far down over his eyes, almost covering his flushed cheeks and concussed expression.

'Bold jumper' does not cover the derring-do of this horse – he can fly like a speeding arrow from the Centaur's bow without so much of an indicative twitch of his long, attentive ears. Never unkind, even so this horse is definitely clumsy on occasion, being the impatient soul that he is. There will be many times when he inadvertently steps on your feet or knocks you into a wall with a cheerful whinny, but don't be upset – it's his Jupiter personality: boisterous, fun-loving and enthusiastic. He is also a gambler (hence the habit of launching joyfully into space) so veterinary insurance is recommended.

Compatible signs: *Aries and Leo*

~ Capricorn ~

(December 22 – January 20)
The sign of the GOAT

Industrious, meticulous, persevering

The horse born a Capricorn is steady, quiet and reliable: an excellent worker. Yet she is not often found in riding schools as might be supposed – oh no, she is too ambitious for that (unless, of course, she is Viennese and has high hopes for a future son). These horses make their slow, determined way to more prestigious positions, perhaps drawing royal carriages or serving conspicuously as regimental drum horses. Like the Goat, the symbol of this sign, she is terrifically sure-footed, so perhaps instead she will be a pack-horse on ground-breaking expeditions.

Whatever she does she will be quietly asserting her indispensability. She won't let you fall or lose your way because, yes, she's a good horse, but essentially her ambition is security. Her satisfaction comes from being useful. Above all other horses, the Capricorn knows the value of a good home and will make sure, if she is pleased with you, that you hang on to her. This is the sign of keeping the 'child's first pony' for the next generation. You will be glad that you did (she will make sure of that) since she tends to improve with age.

Compatible signs: *Taurus and Virgo*